REFLECTIONS ON FAITH INSPIRED BY COVID

Phil Ridden

EDWEST PUBLISHING

Copyright © Phil Ridden, 2020

Published 2020 by Edwest Publishing
Joondalup, Western Australia
www.edwestpublishing.biz

ISBN: Paperback 978-0-9925481-9-3

The author asserts his moral rights.
No part of this publication may be reproduced or transmitted, in any form or by any means without the permission of the author, except for fair use in worship and study.

To contact the author:
Phil@philridden.biz
www.philridden.biz

Cover image (background) by Sasha Freemind on Unsplash.
Cover image (coronavirus) by CDC on Unsplash

CONTENTS

Why this book? iv
Why Covid-19? v
A word about Biblical quotes vi
WASHING HANDS 1
SEPARATION 2
POTS AND PANS 4
TOILET PAPER 6
NAME 8
FIT AND HEALTHY 10
SURVIVAL 12
TEDDY BEARS 14
CHURCH 16
SOCIAL DISTANCE 18
ISOLATION 20
REBELLION 22
HOME SCHOOLING 24
WORDS 26
PASSING IT ON 28
MISLEADING 30
MASKS 32
PLAYGROUNDS 34
DANCING 36
ANXIOUS 38
HOME 40
O MY GOD 42
SINGING 44

EASTER BUNNY	46
MAKESHIFT	48
SELF-INTEREST	50
TOUCH	52
LEADERS	54
HEALING	56
RESTRICTIONS	58
SHIPS	60
GROCERIES ONLINE	62
WHATEVER	64
BREATH	65
NEWS	66
HOPE	68
TURNING	70
RECKLESS	72
NOW	74
KNOCK-ON	76
TRUST	78
PLANS	80
UNSEEN	82
HEROES	84
THE BEST AND THE WORST	86
JOBS	88
CHANGED	90
EASY	92
RECREATION	94
BACK TO SCHOOL	96

SOON	98
HISTORY	100
PRIORITIES	102
OPENING	104
LOCKDOWN	106
SECOND WAVE	108
FACE TO FACE	110
PROTECTED	112
TEST	114
PUBLIC TRANSPORT	115
IT'S OVER	116

Why this book?

More than fifty years ago, Michel Quoist wrote:

> *If we knew how to listen to God, if we knew how to look around us, our whole life would become prayer. ... Words are only a means. However, the silent prayer which has moved beyond words must always spring from everyday life, for everyday life is the raw material of prayer.*[1]

If we seek God, we will see Him revealed in the people and events in our lives.

Including the Covid-19 virus. The impact of the virus on individuals, local communities and the global community can challenge us to think about faith; reveal God to us; and teach us about our relationship with our Eternal Father.

That is the purpose of this book. As you read these reflections, it is likely they will conjure familiar images for you. I hope they will also help you to meditate on God and your relationship with Him.

This is not a book to be read from cover to cover. It is designed to be dipped into, sequentially or not, with favourite passages revisited from time to time. Perhaps it will inspire you to add your own reflections on the theme.

---

[1] Michel Quoist, *Prayers of life*, MH Gill and Sons Ltd, Dublin, 1963, p. 22.

Why Covid-19?

This virus, which carries the unemotive name Covid-19, has impacted a generation of people in ways they had never experienced. Earlier pandemics such as the Bubonic Plague and the Spanish Flu killed many in earlier centuries, but the minor epidemics of this age—polio, ebola, bird flu, SARS, etc.—had more localised or targeted impact. We had known nothing like Covid-19: lockdowns and isolation; closures of schools, shops, churches, even borders; death which showed no discrimination; uncertainty which impacted health, lifestyle, and the economy.

The virus has drawn some people closer to God; challenged the faith of others; confirmed the antagonism of yet others.

Yet we can draw near to God in all circumstances—even in the midst of a pandemic or as we look back on it from the safety of time.

A word about Biblical quotes

A Biblical quote is included for each reflection—yet I do this with a little discomfort. It is too easy to extract verses from their context where they have a particular meaning, and to use them to convey another meaning in a different context. It is possible I have done that in this book—not to give credibility, but to help you to delve into the Bible and to seek out its truth. Forgive me if I've been simplistic. If the Biblical references are helpful, explore them; if not, ignore them.

Contemporary translations have been used. All are available (free of charge) online from various sites.

Bible Translations quoted:

Scripture quotations marked **NIV** are taken from *The Holy Bible: New International Version®*, NIV® Copyright © 1973, 1978, 1984, 2011 by Biblica, Inc.® Used by permission. All rights reserved worldwide.

Scripture quotations marked **GNT** are taken from *Good News Translation®* (Today's English Version, Second Edition), Copyright © 1992 American Bible Society. All rights reserved.

Scripture quotations marked **MSG** are taken from *The Message*. Copyright © 1993, 1994, 1995, 1996, 2000, 2001, 2002. Used by permission of NavPress Publishing Group.

Scripture quotations marked **TLB** are from *The Living Bible* copyright © 1971 by Tyndale House Foundation. Used by permission of Tyndale House Publishers Inc., Carol Stream, Illinois 60188. All rights reserved.

WASHING HANDS

We've been reminded to wash our hands, Father.

Ubiquitous messages tell us
That clean hands
Are essential to health and well-being;
That clean hands
Can help to maintain a clean body,
Free from this virus and other infections;
Keeping sickness from our bodies—
One part of the body
Influencing the health of the whole.

You taught us that, Father—
That a clean heart can keep the whole body clean.
I can wash my hands,
But only you can wash my heart.
So 'Create in me a new, clean heart, O God,
Filled with clean thoughts and right desires.' (Psalm 51:10, TLB)

So let us come near to God with a sincere heart and a sure faith, with hearts that have been purified from a guilty conscience and with bodies washed with clean water. (Hebrews 10: 22, GNT)

SEPARATION

These are isolating times, Father.
>'Stay inside your homes.'
>'Don't go out unless you must.'
>'Don't visit family.'
>'Don't gather.'
>'Don't meet.'
>'Just don't.'

We are separated from people we know and love—
>unable to hold grandchildren,
>unable to share coffee with friends,
>unable to greet church family with a hug,
>unable even to gather to worship you.

I understand it, Father.
I understand the need to prevent this virus spreading;
But I am separated from those I love.

But not from you, Father.
Paul said it so well:

For I am convinced that nothing can ever separate us from his love. Death can't, and life can't. The angels won't, and all the powers of hell itself cannot keep God's love away. Our fears for today, our worries about tomorrow, or where we are—high above the sky, or in the deepest ocean—nothing will ever be able to separate us from the love of God demonstrated by our Lord Jesus Christ when he died for us. (Romans 8: 38–39).

I may feel alone,
>but you are here;

I may be anxious for the future,
    but you are already there;
And nothing can separate me from you—
Nothing.
Nothing.
Nothing.

POTS AND PANS

They're beating pots in the windows, Father.

People are standing in windows and on balconies
Beating saucepans with spoons to make a racket.
It's a call of unity and encouragement
    in a difficult time:
A declaration that I am still strong,
And that you are still strong,
And together we will fight this threat,
And together we will win.

I'm reminded of the siege of Jericho,
When men walked around the walls for seven days
Making noise by beating pots:
A battle cry
That said that together we will win,
If we take God at his word.

A microscopic virus is less intimidated, Father,
But I admire the sentiment.
So often, when things turn against us,
    we withdraw,
    hide even,
    make ourselves small,
    unseen and unheard,
    When we should be bold and visible.

So often, we followers of Christ do it too:
    we try to hide,
    to make ourselves small,
    unseen and unheard,
When we should be bold and visible.

Forgive us, Father.
When your voice needs to be heard,
And we are asked to speak for you,
Make us bold to
    bang on pots,
    sing aloud,
    speak your word,
So that you are heard.

Pray also for me, that whenever I speak, words may be given me so that I will fearlessly make known the mystery of the gospel, for which I am an ambassador in chains. Pray that I may declare it fearlessly, as I should. (Ephesians 6: 19-20, NIV)

TOILET PAPER

They're stripping the shelves of supermarkets, Father.

Driven by fear or greed,
Self-preservation or profiteering,
They create chaos,
    panic,
    insanity.
Showing no care for others—
The slow, aged, disabled, or just courteous—
They are consumed by a reckless grab for what they want:
It's mine!
My needs trump yours!

Why do we behave this way, Father?
Why does the normal, healthy, drive to survive
Morph into greedy and needy,
A grasping obsession
To have what I want,
Irrespective of the needs of others?

I have enough toilet paper, Father.
And yet …
Am I sometimes like this:
Obsessed with my own needs,
    my own desires,
    my own goals,
    my own ambitions,

So that others suffer
In my self-absorbed quest?

Forgive me, Father.
Teach me to love as Jesus loved—
Sacrificially.

And all of you serve each other with humble spirits, for God gives special blessings to those who are humble, but sets himself against those who are proud. If you will humble yourselves under the mighty hand of God, in his good time he will lift you up. Let him have all your worries and cares, for he is always thinking about you and watching everything that concerns you. (1 Peter 5: 5–7, TLB)

NAME

We gave it a name, Father.

At first, we could only speak of
    an unknown illness,
    a virus,
    a coronavirus—
Then we gave it a label, a name:
    Covid-19.
It's clinical,
    scientific,
    not designed to inspire,
    but simply to identify.
Yet, somehow,
The name makes it real,
    authentic,
    gives it substance;
Allows us to understand it,
    to identify related viruses,
    and potential remedies.

So now,
When people ask: What is it?
Then for those who seek to understand,
Its name makes known its character,
    its qualities,
    how we may relate to it,
    and how it relates to us.

Father, God, you have many names:
> Jehovah, I am, Lord Almighty, Holy One, Mighty God, Everlasting Father, Wonderful Counsellor, Prince of Peace, Christ, Messiah, Lamb of God, Son of God, Redeemer, Spirit of God, Spirit of Christ, Spirit of Truth … and more.

When people ask, Who are you?
Then for those who seek to understand.
Your names make known your character
> your qualities,
> how we may relate to you,
> and how you relate to us.

Help me to know you
Through all your names.

GOD, brilliant Lord, yours is a household name. Nursing infants gurgle choruses about you; toddlers shout the songs that drown out enemy talk, and silence atheist babble. I look up at your macro-skies, dark and enormous, your handmade sky-jewellery, moon and stars mounted in their settings. Then I look at my micro-self and wonder, Why do you bother with us? Why take a second look our way? … GOD, brilliant Lord, your name echoes around the world. (Psalm 8: 1-4, 9, MSG)

FIT AND HEALTHY

He died, Father.

The news report said that he was fit and healthy,
Yet his body failed,
    and he passed away,
    quickly.
We had thought this enemy only attacked
    the weak,
    the old,
    the ill,
    the vulnerable.
We understood that.
But now we are confused.
Are we all at risk?
Could we all succumb?

We sometimes think of faith like that, Father.
We like to think that those who follow you,
    earnestly studying your word,
    consistently sharing with your followers,
    diligently listening for your voice,
    faithfully serving your people—
Such people must be safe from sin,
Safe from failing you,
Safe in their faith.

Yet we are each vulnerable,
> easily tempted,
> prone to falter
In our love and service for you.

Let me never be blasé, Father.
Give me a faith that is fit and healthy.
But walk with me
To steer me away from sin,
And lift me when I fall.

It seems to be a fact of life that when I want to do what is right, I inevitably do what is wrong. I love to do God's will so far as my new nature is concerned; but there is something else deep within me, in my lower nature, that is at war with my mind and wins the fight and makes me a slave to the sin that is still within me. In my mind I want to be God's willing servant, but instead I find myself still enslaved to sin. So you see how it is: my new life tells me to do right, but the old nature that is still inside me loves to sin. Oh, what a terrible predicament I'm in! Who will free me from my slavery to this deadly lower nature? Thank God! It has been done by Jesus Christ our Lord. He has set me free. (Romans 7: 21–25, TLB)

SURVIVAL

She survived, Father.

When she was infected with the virus,
Her body fought it,
And won.
She recounted what it was like:
    how she felt, in her body and mind,
    how she suffered,
    how she fought,
    and who sustained her.

Of course, she's not the only one;
But she inspired us,
Reassured us that
    recovery,
    restoration,
    renewal,
Were possible
In the right hands.

We hear stories of faith like this, Father:
Stories of people who have found you,
    who have found forgiveness,
    who have found life.
It inspires us.

It reassures us that
>recovery,
>restoration,
>renewal,

Are possible
In the right hands—
Yours.

Our Saviour Jesus poured out new life so generously. God's gift has restored our relationship with him and given us back our lives. And there's more life to come—an eternity of life! You can count on this. (Titus 3: 6–7, MSG)

TEDDY BEARS

There are teddy bears in the windows, Father.

In the midst of this despair and fear,
Children suffer,
Unable to comprehend the danger,
Yet absorbing the emotions of those around them,
And the gravity of media news.
So teddy bears in the window
    are a message to passing children
That the vitality
    and enthusiasm
    and buoyancy of a child
        pervades this place.
Families set out on bear hunts,
Searching the neighbourhood for teddy bears,
Expressing their elation when one is found,
Infusing them with personalities,
Exchanging greetings,
And imagining their conversation—
Fear stifled by fun.

Thank you for teddy bears, Father:
Symbols of warmth
    and love
    and optimism
    and comfort
    and peace.

Signs of life in the midst of death,
>   of normality in the midst of insanity,
>   of peace in the midst of chaos.

Am I adding to that optimism, Father,
Or am I feeding the fear?

The LORD is my light and my salvation—whom shall I fear? The LORD is the stronghold of my life—of whom shall I be afraid? (Psalm 27: 1, NIV)

CHURCH

We can't go to church, Father.

We cannot gather together
    to worship you,
    to sing your praise,
    to meditate on your word,
    to spend time in conversation with you,
    to reflect on our lives and on you,
    to listen for your voice,
    to share the joys and struggles of friends,
    tell others the good news of Christ,
    and serve them in love ...
I miss that.

Yet we remain Christ's followers.
We do not cease to be the church
If we do not meet.
I do not cease to be part of the church
If I miss a gathering.

I can still worship you,
    sing your praise,
    meditate on your word,
    spend time in conversation with you,
    reflect on my life and on you,
    listen for your voice,
    share the joys and struggles of friends,

> tell others the good news of Christ,
> and serve them in love …

Even from home.

Do I sometimes forget that?
The church has not shut down.
Buildings may be closed,
But your church is still open for business.
We cannot **go** to church,
But we can continue to **be** the church,
No matter how locked down we are.

We are pressed on every side by troubles, but we are not crushed. We are perplexed, but not driven to despair. We are hunted down, but never abandoned by God. We get knocked down, but we are not destroyed. Through suffering, our bodies continue to share in the death of Jesus so that the life of Jesus may also be seen in our bodies. (2 Corinthians 4: 8–10, TLB)

SOCIAL DISTANCE

We have to maintain a safe distance, Father.

It's uncomfortable.
When we meet with family and friends,
We need to touch,
    to embrace,
    to kiss;
    at the very least to shake hands.
We are social beings.
We supplement our verbal communication
    with body language
    and touch—
Or perhaps we supplement our body language and touch
    with words …
But, for now,
We must stand apart,
Keeping a safe distance.

It's not really new, Father.
There are many people in our community
We like to keep at a safe distance—
    the homeless,
    the hungry,
    the dirty,
    the alcoholic,
    the drug addict …
They make us uncomfortable,
Held at arm's length

To avoid communication—
> the sorrowful eyes,
> the imploring hands,
> the beseeching words.

Am I guilty of this, Father:
Ignoring those in need of help,
> in need of a kind word,
> in need of compassion,
> in need of **my** help and words and compassion,

And your love?

I was hungry and you fed me, I was thirsty and you gave me a drink, I was homeless and you gave me a room, I was shivering and you gave me clothes, I was sick and you stopped to visit, I was in prison and you came to me. … Whenever you did one of these things to someone overlooked or ignored, that was me—you did it to me. (Matthew 25: 35–40, MSG)

ISOLATION

We're isolated, Father.
Locked down,
Confined to our homes,
    or hotels,
    or ships,
    or wherever we are;
Discouraged from meeting with others;
Leaving homes only for essential purposes.

It's not who we are.
You created us to be social beings,
To have relationships with others,
To share with them
    our love and care and compassion,
    our joy and exhilaration,
    our pain and grief;
Not to withdraw into ourselves,
Away from others.
Father, even in our physical isolation,
Draw us into community with one another.

You created is to be in a relationship with you,
To share with you
    our love and care and compassion,
    our joy and exhilaration,
    our pain and grief.

Yet we isolate ourselves,
Draw away from you,
Deprive ourselves of that relationship.

Do I isolate myself from you, Father?
Do I avoid meeting you,
    connecting with you,
    conversing with you?
And when we meet,
Do I limit our relationship with formality,
A cursory greeting
Restrained by formal prayers and awkward phrases
    learned from others?

Break through my isolation, Father.
Draw me into communion with you.

Is there anyplace I can go to avoid your Spirit? to be out of your sight? If I climb to the sky, you're there! If I go underground, you're there! If I flew on morning's wings to the far western horizon, You'd find me in a minute—you're already there waiting! (Psalm 139: 7-10, MSG)

REBELLION

Some people reject the messages, Father.

The government and health officials,
Seeking to curb the proliferation of this virus,
Are sending clear directions:
    No large gatherings.
    Places where people meet socially are closed.
    Maintain a safe distance from others.

Yet some laugh and reject the message:
    'We are not paranoid;
    We are invincible;
    The rules are not for us.'

You understand this, don't you Father?
People have rejected your messages
In every generation
Since the beginning of time—
    messages recorded in the Bible;
    messages relayed by prophets;
    messages shared by Jesus;
    messages still heard today.

Do I close my ears to your messages, Father?
When I want to do my own thing
And not yours,
Do I ignore your voice?

Your ears are open but you don't hear a thing. Your eyes are awake but you don't see a thing. The people are blockheads! They stick their fingers in their ears so they won't have to listen; They screw their eyes shut so they won't have to look, so they won't have to deal with me face-to-face and let me heal them. But you have God-blessed eyes—eyes that see! And God-blessed ears—ears that hear! (Matthew 13: 14–16, MSG)

HOME SCHOOLING

We're home schooling, Father.

Schools have been forced to close their doors,
So teachers have adapted,
Moved online,
    delivering lessons,
    setting work,
    tutoring students,
    reporting to parents,
With video clips,
    face to face meetings,
        and other technologies;
Teachers, students, parents
Simply adapting,
As needs must.

Even your church has been forced to close doors,
So your people
Have adapted,
Moved online,
And into carparks and drive-throughs,
To share your love.

Will you help me to adapt, Father—
To find new ways
    to share your good news,
    teach others of your love,
    tell the story of Jesus?

Will you help me,
>	amid new and evolving circumstances,
>	wrestling with new demands
>	in a new world,
To share your message anew.

All these new things are from God who brought us back to himself through what Christ Jesus did. And God has given us the privilege of urging everyone to come into his favour and be reconciled to him. For God was in Christ, restoring the world to himself, no longer counting men's sins against them but blotting them out. This is the wonderful message he has given us to tell others. (2 Corinthians 5: 19–20, TLB)

WORDS

There have been some stirring words, Father.

Some leaders have been honest about the virus,
    frank about the threat,
    sensitive about the difficulty,
    encouraging about the outcome,
    inspirational about the challenge;
Convincing us that we can stay safe
If we do as we are implored to do—
And people have responded.

Words are powerful, Father.
When the right words,
    from the right people,
    at the right time,
    are delivered in the right way,
People respond.

They responded to Jesus, too:
To his words of compassion
    and truth,
    and inspiration,
    and love;
Pointing the way to you.

Are my words like that, Father?
Do my words lift people?
Do my words point them to you?

On hearing it, many of his disciples said, 'This is a hard teaching. Who can accept it?' ... From this time many of his disciples turned back and no longer followed him. 'You do not want to leave too, do you?' Jesus asked the Twelve. Simon Peter answered him, 'Lord, to whom shall we go? You have the words of eternal life.' (John 6: 60, 66–68, NIV)

PASSING IT ON

We are careful not to pass the virus on, Father.

If we touch things—
    door knobs,
    shopping trolleys,
    supermarket items,
    benchtops,
    remote controls,
    phones …
Then we may pass this virus to others—
Unknowingly,
As a link in a chain of contact.
We have a responsibility
    to avoid
        passing it on to others.

We can pass your love on too, Father:
If we touch people—
    their lives,
    their hearts,
    their minds,
    their dreams,
    their hopes …
Then we may pass your love to them—
Unknowingly,
As a link in a chain of contact.
Am I playing my part in the chain, Father,
Passing your love on to others?

The sacred writings contain preliminary reports by the prophets on God's Son. His descent from David roots him in history; his unique identity as Son of God was shown by the Spirit when Jesus was raised from the dead, setting him apart as the Messiah, our Master. Through him we received both the generous gift of his life and the urgent task of passing it on to others who receive it by entering into obedient trust in Jesus. You are who you are through this gift and call of Jesus Christ!
(Romans 1: 2–6, MSG)

MISLEADING

People are spreading dangerous lies, Father.

Social media is rife
With dangerous and unfounded remedies
Which claim to cure or prevent this virus:
    drink water;
    gargle with salt and vinegar;
    inject disinfectant;
    drink antiseptic.
Hundreds died from fake remedies.
Are the disseminators naïve
Or intentionally destructive?

There is no shortage of charlatans,
    who mislead others,
    for gain or sadistic pleasure.
Jesus spoke against such people,
Warning of skilled deceivers
    who delight in leading us astray,
Even in matters of faith.

Make me discerning, Father,
Able to recognise those who would point to paths
That lead away from your love.
For I want always
To stay close to you.

Beware of false teachers who come disguised as harmless sheep, but are wolves and will tear you apart. You can detect them by the way they act, just as you can identify a tree by its fruit. You need never confuse grapevines with thorn bushes or figs with thistles. Different kinds of fruit trees can quickly be identified by examining their fruit. A variety that produces delicious fruit never produces an inedible kind. And a tree producing an inedible kind can't produce what is good. So the trees having the inedible fruit are chopped down and thrown on the fire. Yes, the way to identify a tree or a person is by the kind of fruit produced. (Matthew 7: 15–20, TLB)

MASKS

Many people are wearing masks, Father.

The official advice is mixed.
Some say we should wear masks
    whenever we are near other people.
Others say that the masks add nothing,
    if social distancing is heeded.
But many wear them anyway,
Cautiously adding whatever protection they can,
To the measures already in place.

We're used to wearing masks, Father—
Invisible masks
    that hide our authentic selves;
    that protect our insecure selves;
    that screen our secret selves;
    that portray the persona we want to show;
    that allow us to be the person
        we want others to believe we are.

There are no masks with you, Father.
You know who I am—
    in weakness and in strength,
    in vulnerability and confidence.

I'm glad that with you there is no pretext.
I am who I am.
But am I also who you created me to be?

LORD, you have examined me and you know me. You know everything I do; from far away you understand all my thoughts. You see me, whether I am working or resting; you know all my actions. Even before I speak, you already know what I will say. You are all around me on every side; you protect me with your power. Your knowledge of me is too deep; it is beyond my understanding. (Psalm 139: 1–6, GNT)

PLAYGROUNDS

They've closed the playgrounds, Father.

Kids can no longer go into the park
    to swing,
    to slide,
    to climb,
    to dangle,
    to throw and kick and hit balls,
    to throw frisbees,
To play with unrestrained joy,
Challenging themselves to achieve new skills and confidence.

You gave them hearts
    to laugh
    and to find simple joys in playful activities.

You also gave me a heart
    to laugh
    and to find simple joys in playful activities.
Do I find play in your service, Father?
Do I serve with unrestrained joy,
Challenging myself to achieve new skills and confidence,
In a life filled to overflowing by you?
Or might the playground just as well be shut down?

What shall I say about this nation? These people are like children playing, who say to their little friends, 'We played wedding and you weren't happy, so we played funeral but you weren't sad.' For John the Baptist doesn't even drink wine and often goes without food, and you say, 'He's crazy.' And I, the Messiah, feast and drink, and you complain that I am 'a glutton and a drinking man, and hang around with the worst sort of sinners!' But brilliant men like you can justify your every inconsistency! (Matthew 11: 16–19, TLB)

DANCING

They're dancing, Father, and posting it online.

It began with one isolated family
Performing bizarre dance routines,
For the enjoyment of others.
It was not skilled,
But it was entertaining—
And that was the point.
Now the videos proliferate:
    families
    workmates,
    emergency workers,
Dancing for our entertainment.

Some people have a resilient spirit, Father.
Circumstances which cause some to despair
Cause others to blossom,
Finding joy in little things.
When we find ourselves falling,
Some people splat—
    remain on the ground, shattered;
Others bounce,
    lifting to new heights of elation.

Is my faith resilient, Father?
With you
    every day is new,

every moment an opportunity,
every event a possibility,
every blessing a reminder of your abundant love,
every setback a lesson in trusting you.
Yet sometimes, I allow myself to splat.
Remind me always of the higher heights and greater joys that await
When I bounce back into your arms,
Content in the knowledge
That I live in your care.

I know what it is to be in need and what it is to have more than enough. I have learned this secret, so that anywhere, at any time, I am content, whether I am full or hungry, whether I have too much or too little. I have the strength to face all conditions by the power that Christ gives me. (Philippians 4: 12–13, GNT)

ANXIOUS

Our children are anxious, Father.

Their normality has been disrupted:
    schooling from home;
    parents out of work;
And on the TV,
    reports of illness and death;
    hospitals overwhelmed;
    scenes of panic in shops;
        uncertainty,
        fear,
        despair,
        political posturing and accusation.
They are powerless to even understand,
    let alone to have any impact,
And many are anxious.

Father, our children are infected,
By the anxiety-virus;
Infected by us—
    our hope,
    our confidence,
    our belief,
    our ability
        to cope,
        to carry on,
        to survive,

      to persist,
      to find a way forward.

Yet how can we fear,
When our hope is in you?
Help us to teach our children **that** hope.

The Lord is my light and my salvation—whom shall I fear? The Lord is the stronghold of my life—of whom shall I be afraid? (Psalm 27: 1, NIV)

HOME

We're told to stay home, Father.

I'm not troubled.
I like my home.
Here in my space,
My life is infused
    with my things,
    my comforts,
    my entertainment,
    my food,
    my family.
Why would I object to staying home?
On dreary days at work,
    I long to go home.
When leave is due,
    I long for weeks at home.
When I've worked too much overtime,
    I long for a day at home.

Some Christians can't wait to go 'home' to you.
Me, Father, not so much.
When the time is right,
    I look forward to being home with you.
But right now,
I am content at home with you
    here;

Because if home is where the heart is,
Then home is anywhere you are,
And you are always with me.
So wherever I am on this planet,
    or any other,
I am home.

Your goodness and unfailing kindness shall be with me all of my life, and afterwards I will live with you forever in your home. (Psalm 23: 6, TLB.)

O MY GOD

In crisis we turn to you, Father.

We do it unconsciously—
> in pain,
> in deep distress,
> in desperation;
> in joy,
> in exuberance,
> in exhilaration.

Whether or not we acknowledge you in our lives,
We find ourselves saying
'Oh my God', 'Jesus', 'Christ':
Unconsciously,
Unthinkingly,
Unwittingly—
> but not unhopefully—

We call your name,
Because you have planted deep within us
A need to connect with you.
So in our extreme, unedited moments,
We call to you.

Thank you that you wait patiently for me,
And whenever I am ready,
You are there.

And we are sure of this, that he will listen to us whenever we ask him for anything in line with his will. And if we really know he is listening when we talk to him and make our requests, then we can be sure that he will answer us. (1 John 5: 14–15, TLB)

SINGING

He sang for the neighbourhood, Father.

He was an opera singer,
Wanting to bring cheer to his neighbours,
Isolated for their safety.
So he stood on the back of a truck,
There in the street,
And accompanied by a musician,
    he sang.
Residents stood outside to applaud.
Then he moved on to another location.

Thinking creatively,
He used the talent he had,
And in so doing brought joy,
Surprising everyone,
With his gift
And his generosity.

Do I do that enough, Father?
Do I creatively seek ways
To use the gifts I have,
To bring joy,
To share your love?

Love is patient and kind; it is not jealous or conceited or proud; love is not ill-mannered or selfish or irritable; love does not keep a record of wrongs; love is not happy with evil, but is happy with the truth. Love never gives up; and its faith, hope, and patience never fail. (1 Corinthians 13: 4–7, TLB)

EASTER BUNNY

The Easter Bunny will come, they said, Father.

That's what they told the children,
While we were in lockdown,
Isolated in our homes,
Hiding away from sight
Because of potential danger.
They reassured the children that
The Easter bunny would find them
To surprise and excite,
And infuse the children with wonder and amazement.

It reminds me that, after Easter,
Your disciples went into lockdown,
Hiding away from sight,
Because of potential danger.
Then you appeared,
Reassured them that you had come,
To surprise and excite.
And infuse the disciples with wonder and amazement.

You still come, Father,
When we are locked down in fear and trepidation,
To reassure us of your presence,
To surprise and excite,
And infuse our lives with wonder and amazement.

Praise the Lord, my soul! All my being, praise his holy name! Praise the Lord, my soul, and do not forget how kind he is. He forgives all my sins and heals all my diseases. He keeps me from the grave and blesses me with love and mercy. He fills my life with good things, so that I stay young and strong like an eagle. (Psalm 103: 1–5, GNT)

MAKESHIFT

They're erecting makeshift hospitals, Father.

In some cities,
    thousands are ill,
    hospitals are overwhelmed,
    beds are jumbled into corridors and storerooms.
So they are constructing field hospitals.

Lacking the accoutrements,
    the design beauty,
    the technology,
    the ornaments,
    the space,
Of established buildings,
Inspired workers meet the need,
Using their gifts and their compassion,
And whatever tools they have,
To bring healing.

It reminds me of the church, Father.
In some places,
Thousands are spiritually ill,
So people gather in field churches,
    under trees or rough shelters,
    in homes or sheds.
Lacking the accoutrements,
    the design beauty,
    the technology,

      the ornaments,
      the space,
Of established buildings,
Inspired workers meet the need,
Using their gifts and compassion,
And whatever tools they have,
To bring healing.

Do we worry too much about buildings, Father?
Do we put too much focus on the façade
And too little on what happens inside—
Inside the building,
Inside our hearts?

The teacher of religion replied, 'Sir, you have spoken a true word in saying that there is only one God and no other. And I know it is far more important to love him with all my heart and understanding and strength, and to love others as myself, than to offer all kinds of sacrifices on the altar of the Temple.' (Mark 12: 32–33, TLB)

SELF-INTEREST

His self-interest troubles me, Father.

He had 1800 rolls of toilet paper,
    and he asked the shop to buy them back.
I can only assume that he bought them to resell,
    at an exorbitant profit.
But there is no longer a shortage—
    was no shortage.
The panic buying is over,
And he is left with 1800 rolls.

I thought:
Serves him right;
He got his just desserts;
He exacerbated a problem
    hoping to profit from it.
The shop manager simply answered him
    with a gesture!

Is it entrepreneurship,
    opportunism,
    or greed?
Why are some so quick to seize a chance
To gain from difficult circumstances,
To exploit the situation while others struggle?

And yet, in my judgement of others,
Am I blind to my own weaknesses, Father?

Do I justify my own self-interest?
Do I love as you require?
Do I live as you require?

Where there is jealousy and selfishness, there is also disorder and every kind of evil. But the wisdom from above is pure first of all; it is also peaceful, gentle, and friendly; it is full of compassion and produces a harvest of good deeds; it is free from prejudice and hypocrisy. And goodness is the harvest that is produced from the seeds the peacemakers plant in peace. (James 3: 16–18, GNT)

TOUCH

They touch through the glass, Father.

Old folk,
Isolated for their safety,
Longing to hold
    a child,
    a grandchild,
    a friend,
Place a hand on the window.
It is mirrored by a hand on the other side,
And so they 'touch'.
It's not the same as a hug—
    they cannot feel the warmth,
    cannot hear whispered words of love—
But it helps.

You and I do that, Father.
Sometimes I feel your arms around me;
Feel the warmth of your touch;
Hear you whisper in my ear.
At other times,
I feel 'out of touch',
Unable to experience that warmth.

I know you haven't left me.
You still reach out,
But I have created a window,
A piece of glass,

A barrier between us.

So as I reach to touch the glass, Father,
Will you touch the other side?
Because the warmth of your love,
Will melt the glass,
And bring us in touch again.

We ask our God to make you worthy of the life he has called you to live. May he fulfil by his power all your desire for goodness and complete your work of faith. In this way the name of our Lord Jesus will receive glory from you, and you from him, by the grace of our God and of the Lord Jesus Christ. (2 Thessalonians 1: 11–12, GNT)

LEADERS

I am grateful for leaders, Father—
    well, some of them.

Leaders in government, community, health,
Have guided us through this coronavirus maze,
Even though they have never been here before,
    to rehearse the journey,
    scout the terrain,
    glimpse the ending.

Yet many have modelled
Collaboration,
    sharing the best of ideas;
Creativity,
    seeking imaginative solutions;
Caution,
    showing respect for the dangers ahead;
Compassion,
    supporting those suffer and grieve;
Composure,
    sensitively responding to criticisms and uncertainty;
Consistency,
    showing the behaviours they expect of others.

You gave us leaders, Father.
Thank you for leaders
Who follow your leading.

And because leaders do not need titles
To lead when a leader is needed,
Will you help me to lead
If I am needed?

When I was beleaguered and bitter, totally consumed by envy, I was totally ignorant, a dumb ox in your very presence. I'm still in your presence, but you've taken my hand. You wisely and tenderly lead me, and then you bless me. (Psalm 73: 21–24, MSG)

HEALING

We admire the health workers, Father.

They model sacrifice:
Working long hours;
Persisting through exhaustion;
Watching people die despite best knowledge and effort;
Unable to take enough time to vent their own distress,
    or to respond to the anguish of loved ones;
Selflessly risking their own health;
Some succumbing to the infection themselves,
    and suffering—
    dying—
Because of a commitment to serve.

In gratitude,
In some communities,
People stand in their doorways each evening
    and applaud,
Their gift of gratitude appreciated,
Even if the sounds of death and sickness drown it out.

Jesus reached out to those who were ill:
Some with no hope of cure,
    who relied on family or begging to survive;
Some whom society had banished,
    outcasts condemned to isolation.

Through your healing,
> you enabled them to return to life,
> and to community.

You understand sickness and pain and rejection.
You understand how it impacts us all.

I am not a doctor, Father.
I have no skills or knowledge to heal others.
Yet I can have compassion;
I can show care;
I can gift encouragement.
Do I do it enough?
And will you help me?

Jesus went all over Galilee, teaching in the synagogues, preaching the Good News about the Kingdom, and healing people who had all kinds of disease and sickness. The news about him spread through the whole country of Syria, so that people brought to him all those who were sick, suffering from all kinds of diseases and disorders: people with demons, and epileptics, and paralytics—and Jesus healed them all. (Matthew 4: 23–24, GNT)

RESTRICTIONS

We seem to be so restricted, Father.

Bounded,
Limited,
In where we can go,
    what we can do,
    who we can meet,
    how we can relate.

Life itself feels restricted,
As though we are not fully able to be
    the people we want to be,
    the people we were created to be.

But there are other things that restrict our lives, Father:
A focus on ourselves,
    our own needs and desires,
    our obsessions and passions;
The absence of you.

The restrictions will lift,
Our freedoms will return,
Coffee shops will reopen,
We will feel release,
And life will be fulfilling.

Thank you that I have found that freedom now—
A life that's free and fulfilled—
In you.

You can readily recall, can't you, how at one time the more you did just what you felt like doing—not caring about others, not caring about God—the worse your life became and the less freedom you had? And how much different is it now as you live in God's freedom, your lives healed and expansive in holiness? (Romans 6: 19, MSG)

SHIPS

We opened our doors to trouble, Father.

The ship arrived in our port,
With travellers showing symptoms of this virus.
Health warnings and advice were somehow ignored,
And we opened the doors,
Allowing them into the community.
The consequence was immediate and traumatic—
> infection;
> death.

It is right that we should have shown compassion
> and provided care;
But we were careless
In protecting our community
From things that would infect our bodies,
And damage our health.

We are also sometimes careless, Father,
In protecting our community
From things that would infect our minds
> and our hearts,
And damage our mental health,
> our emotional health,
> our moral health,
> our spiritual health;
Our lives
> and our relationships.

Reflections on faith inspired by Covid   Phil Ridden

Am I sometimes careless, Father,
In protecting myself
From things that would infect my mind
    And my heart,
And damage my life
    and my relationship
        with you?
Help me, Father, to protect the borders of my heart.

Keep vigilant watch over your heart; that's where life starts.
(Proverbs 4: 23, MSG)

GROCERIES ONLINE

We're shopping for groceries online, Father.

It's a new experience.
In the shop,
    we locate items by habit,
    moving up and down the aisles,
    selecting familiar items as we see them,
    following a routinised search pattern.
But online,
    we must search for items,
    chasing up and down the site,
    hoping to recognise familiar items as we see them,
    creating a randomised search pattern.
We place our order,
Online,
    to fill our pantry,
    to fill our life with good things.
Substitutions are not acceptable.

And our requests are met:
Delivered to the door,
As we ordered—
    well almost;
When promised—
    well almost;
Everything we needed—
    well almost:
There's always something we overlooked!

Some people think of prayer this way, Father:
Placing an order with you
Online,
Describing in detail
    what they want
    what they expect
    and when.
Substitutions are not acceptable.

But you, Father God,
Creator and Lord over all things,
Are not our online shop,
Supplying our wants to order.
It is our task to meet your expectations,
Not your task to meet ours.
And yet …
You listen when I call;
You supply my needs;
You fill my life with good things.

And with all his abundant wealth through Christ Jesus, my God will supply all your needs. To our God and Father be the glory forever and ever! Amen. (Philippians 4: 20, GNT)

WHATEVER

This waiting for results is stressful, Father.

I'm not patient at the best of times,
But now I wait to know
If I have the virus,
Or if those I love have the virus.
How do I wait,
Knowing that this could change my life,
Could take my life,
Or theirs …?

Our young folk have a word
To dismiss consequences or uncertainty:
They say:
  'Whatever',
A simple word that banishes fear …
Sometimes.

As I wait, Father,
Will you sit with me?
Will you strengthen me to face the outcome?
Will you give me peace?
  Whatever ….?

I waited and waited and waited for GOD. At last he looked; finally he listened. He lifted me out of the ditch, pulled me from deep mud. He stood me up on a solid rock to make sure I wouldn't slip. He taught me how to sing the latest God-song, a praise-song to our God. (Psalm 40: 1–3, MSG)

BREATH

There are screens on the shop counters, Father.

Clear screens,
Shielding us from shop assistants,
So that we don't breathe on them
And they don't breathe on us.
The masks perform the same purpose,
Blocking the breath of others,
Breath that may bring us death.

But yours is the breath of life, Father.
You inspire us,
Breathing your Spirit into us,
Your breath giving us life.

It stands to reason, doesn't it, that if the alive-and-present God who raised Jesus from the dead moves into your life, he'll do the same thing in you that he did in Jesus, bringing you alive to himself? When God lives and breathes in you (and he does, as surely as he did in Jesus), you are delivered from that dead life. With his Spirit living in you, your body will be as alive as Christ's! (Romans 8: 10–11, MSG)

NEWS

News dominates our lives, Father.

What is the latest about the virus?
How many have died?
How many new cases are there?
What are the new rules?
Is there any lifting of restrictions?
Have we found a vaccine?
Are we winning?

Yet, despite our curiosity, our interest quickly wanes.
If there is nothing to stir our emotions—
>images of people suffering,
>or weeping for loved ones,
>or protesting,
>or ignoring the rules;
>something to get us excited,
>something to get us reacting,
>something to have us talking—

Then we tire of
>the same reports,
>the same predictions,
>the same images,

Dressed up to look new,
As journalists look for something to report.

Are we like that with your news, Father?
You have the Good News,
The story of Jesus—

how you love us,
how you sent Jesus to be one of us,
how he died to open the pathway to you,
how he rose again to conquer death,
how he urged his followers to tell the story anew,
how you gave us your Spirit to continue with us.
Let me never tire of hearing this news,
Or telling it.

After John had been put in prison, Jesus went to Galilee and preached the Good News from God. 'The right time has come,' he said, 'and the Kingdom of God is near! Turn away from your sins and believe the Good News!' (Mark 1: 14–15, GNT)

HOPE

I love the stories of hope, Father.

They are told on the news,
    seen in the paper,
    shared online.
Stories of people
Inspiring others,
Displacing fear with hope.

Love is your first name, Father;
Hope is your second.
In you there is always hope—
Hope that we will survive;
Hope that a vaccine will be found;
Hope that life will return to normal.

And beyond this moment in time—
Hope in this world for a fulfilling life.
Hope in the next world for eternal life.

Keep me strong in my hope, Father,
And in sharing that hope with others.

I saw the Lord before me at all times; he is near me, and I will not be troubled. And so I am filled with gladness, and my words are full of joy. And I, mortal though I am, will rest assured in hope, because you will not abandon me in the world of the dead; you will not allow your faithful servant to rot in the grave. You have shown me the paths that lead to life, and your presence will fill me with joy. (Acts 2: 25–28, GNT)

Let your hope keep you joyful, be patient in your troubles, and pray at all times. (Romans 12: 12, GNT)

TURNING

The people have had enough of lockdowns, Father.

When told to go into isolation,
    to maintain social distancing,
    to avoid crowded places,
They saw the wisdom and (mostly) obeyed.

But now they have turned:
'We did what you said;
    but now we've had enough.
You said we will get sick and die;
    but I'm OK and so are my friends.
You said isolation would solve the problem;
    but people have still been infected.
You want us to live like this indefinitely;
    but we need our friends.
We expected that you would conquer this thing;
    but you haven't, so we no longer trust you.'

They are fickle,
Impatient,
Lacking perseverance and resilience.

Am I like that, Father,
In my service for you?
Do I tire and lose resolve with time?
Do I give up when nothing seems to change?
Do I weaken when my plans don't bear fruit?

Happy are those who remain faithful under trials, because when they succeed in passing such a test, they will receive as their reward the life which God has promised to those who love him. (James 1: 12, GNT)

RECKLESS

Some people have a reckless confidence, Father.

They gather with friends,
    ignore distancing rules,
    neglect washing hands,
    breach self-isolation demands,
    scorn authorities who impose restrictions.
They have a reckless confidence in science,
    in the strength of their bodies,
    in science's ability to protect them
        and save them.

Christians do it too.
Some hold worship services,
    ignore distancing rules
    neglect washing hands,
    breach self-isolation demands,
    scorn authorities who impose restrictions.
They have a reckless confidence in you,
    in the strength of their faith,
    in your ability and willingness to protect them
        and save them.

Help me to discern, Father,
The time for caution,
And the time for confidence,
And the danger in arrogance.

But through it all,
Give me the faith that Martin Luther spoke of—
A lively, reckless confidence in your grace.

Then Jesus called the children over to him and said to the disciples, 'Let the little children come to me! Never send them away! For the Kingdom of God belongs to men who have hearts as trusting as these little children's. And anyone who doesn't have their kind of faith will never get within the Kingdom's gates.' (Luke 18: 16–17, TLB)

NOW

They're calling for the borders to open, Father.

It's affecting the economy;
It's preventing the football from restarting;
It's affecting people's mental health.
And anyway,
It's no longer necessary.
People are not getting sick.
We must be over it.
We need to get back to normal.

They may be right—
They may not.
Who can know what the consequences will be?
We have trusted our leaders,
Because they see the big picture;
They have the plan.

But we are impatient people.
We do not like our lifestyle restricted;
We want what makes us happy;
We expect the freedom to do what we want to do—
Now.

I think sometimes I'm impatient in my faith, Father.
I prayed for the drought to break—
Now.
I prayed for the bushfires to be halted—

Now.
I prayed that I would get a job—
Now.
I prayed for the child to be made well—
Now.
I prayed for my friend to find you—
Now.
I prayed for world leaders to work together in peace—
Now.
How much longer must I wait?
How much longer?
How long … ?

Help me, Father,
To trust you.
Because you see the big picture;
You have the plan.
I will wait.
Help me to be patient—
(Now …)

Relent, LORD! How long will it be? Have compassion on your servants. Satisfy us in the morning with your unfailing love, that we may sing for joy and be glad all our days. (Psalm 90: 13–14, NIV)

KNOCK-ON

This virus has a knock-on effect, Father.

It began by affecting our health.
So restrictions were imposed
    on travel,
    socialising,
    working,
    school,
    shopping,
    gyms,
    beauticians,
    coffee shops,
    church,
    funerals,
    weddings …
The restrictions were endless.

But this affected the economy:
    employment,
    businesses,
    the share market,
    housing prices,
    superannuation,
    livelihoods …

And this affected the mental health
    of those who cannot cope with isolation,
    or the fear of uncertainty …

And the safety of those who were victims
    of domestic violence …

We began with one issue,
But as we dealt with that, others emerged.
We were reminded that
No individual stands alone;
    each influences others.
No action stands alone;
    each has consequences.
No decision stands alone;
    each has a knock-on effect,
Like falling dominoes or books.

That's how sin is, Father.
One step
    leads to another
        and another,
Until we are consumed.
Keep me safe, Father,
From actions and people and decisions
That would tumble one upon another,
Beyond my ability to resist.

Beware that in your plenty you don't forget the Lord your God and begin to disobey him. For when you have become full and prosperous and have built fine homes to live in, and when your flocks and herds have become very large, and your silver and gold have multiplied, that is the time to watch out that you don't become proud and forget the Lord your God. (Deuteronomy 8: 11–14, TLB)

TRUST

We are losing trust in our abilities, Father.

Why is this thing still here?
Why have our scientists not created a vaccine?
Why has the government not solved this?
We are human—one step below God!
We have solved the mysteries of the universe,
    the mysteries of the planet,
    the mysteries of our bodies,
    the mysteries of our minds.
There is nothing we cannot achieve.
So why is this thing still haunting us?
Who is holding us back?
Who is to blame?
Who can we trust?

Who can we trust?
Only you, Father.
There is much we do not know:
We can send probes to distant planets,
Design computers to process unlimited data,
Watch events as they happen across the world—
Yet we are outwitted by a microscopic virus.
We trust in our own knowledge,
    our own wisdom,
    our own goodness.
But in you, Father,
In you alone,

Just in you,
Can we really trust.

Don't put your trust in human leaders; no human being can save you. When they die, they return to the dust; on that day all their plans come to an end. Happy are those who have the God of Jacob to help them and who depend on the LORD their God, the Creator of heaven, earth, and sea, and all that is in them. (Psalm 146: 3–6, GNT)

PLANS

They've spent years preparing, Father.

These elite athletes have trained,
    tested their limits,
    focused their time and energy,
    prioritised one goal above all else:
To compete in the 2020 Tokyo Olympics.
But now they have learned
They will not travel,
    nor gather with fellow athletes,
    nor compete in this prestigious event,
    nor achieve the goals they anticipated.
Their plans,
    ambitions,
    hopes,
Will remain unfulfilled—
At least, for now.
Because suddenly,
    unexpectedly
Circumstances have changed,
    opportunities have evaporated,
        dreams have been dashed,

So often, Father,
    we plan,
    strive,
    prioritise one goal above all others;

And then, suddenly,
    unexpectedly,
Circumstances change
    opportunities evaporate,
        dreams are dashed.

It is good to make plans,
Conjure dreams and ambitions,
And pursue them with our bodies and hearts;
But Father,
Do I prioritise my plans above yours?
Do I seek my own glory before yours?
Do I relegate you to the back seat so I can drive?

Help me, Father,
To honour the skills you gave me,
To fulfil the call you have for me.

In everything you do, put God first, and he will direct you and crown your efforts with success. (Proverbs 3: 6, TLB)

UNSEEN

This enemy is unseen, Father.

This enemy that stalks us
Is invisible, strong and unknown:
It is microscopic,
> so we cannot see to avoid it.

It is pervasive,
> present on surfaces and in the air.

It is powerful,
> so that even the strong succumb.

For a time, we didn't even know what to call it.
So we have no weapons,
> no defences,
> no agreed expectations.

Yet it is real.
It lurks in shadows, but attacks in the light.
We fight as we might subdue a tiger with a feather.

It's not unlike evil, Satan, the devil—
Whatever name we call him.
The enemy stalks us,
Steals into our lives,
Initially undetected,
Until it begins to do its damage,
To change our hearts,
> our thoughts,
> our actions.

Reflections on faith inspired by Covid   Phil Ridden

Keep me safe, Father,
From sickness that will destroy me—
Sickness of the body,
And sickness of the soul.

Be careful—watch out for attacks from Satan, your great enemy. He prowls around like a hungry, roaring lion, looking for some victim to tear apart. Stand firm when he attacks. Trust the Lord; and remember that other Christians all around the world are going through these sufferings too. (1 Peter 5: 8–9, TLB)

HEROES

We're learning about heroes, Father.

So often, those we raise,
    and praise,
As heroes;
Those we decorate
    and emulate,
As holders of the truth,
Let us down.

We honour them because they have a talent
    as entertainers,
    sports-people,
    performers;
But their self-indulgence leads to
    dissipation,
    degradation,
    dissoluteness.

Yet, little by little,
    we have seen change.
During these days of isolation,
We have seen heroes,
Sacrificing
    their health,
    their time,
    their own comfort,
    their well-being,
For others.

Instead of obsessing about celebrities,
We have celebrated lives worth celebrating,
    honoured lives worth honouring,
    commended lives worth commending.

Any of us can be a hero, Father—
Perhaps unknown,
    unheralded,
    unacknowledged,
But understanding sacrifice,
    and compassion,
    and hopefulness,
    and service.

When a hero is needed, Father,
By the community or by you,
Do I respond,
Or am I left standing,
Hoping someone else will step forward?

If any of you wants to serve me, then follow me. Then you'll be where I am, ready to serve at a moment's notice. The Father will honour and reward anyone who serves me. (John 12: 26, MSG)

THE BEST AND THE WORST

Times like this bring out our best and our worst, Father.

We've seen the worst already:
People grabbing at household supplies
    with no thought for the needs of others;
Or refusing to cooperate with those
    who are trying to minimise the transfer of infection—
People driven by their own wants.

But we're also seeing the best, Father:
Young people shopping for the elderly,
    leaving supplies on doorsteps;
An opera singer singing in the street,
    to entertain the neighbourhood;
A convoy of vehicles passing the home of a child,
    to celebrate their birthday;
Neighbours greeting one another over the fence,
    to bring companionship and encouragement;
Health workers, with no thought for their own safety,
    working long hours to save the sick—
People driven by others' needs.

You bring out the best in us, Father.
Jesus changed our world with his love,
And Paul described that love eloquently:
Love is patient and kind; it is not jealous or conceited or proud;
love is not ill-mannered or selfish or irritable; love does not
keep a record of wrongs; love is not happy with evil, but is

happy with the truth. Love never gives up; and its faith, hope, and patience never fail. (1 Corinthians 13: 4–7, GNT)

Will you help me to love with this love?
Will you bring out the best in me?

Yes, God will give you much so that you can give away much, and when we take your gifts to those who need them they will break out into thanksgiving and praise to God for your help. So two good things happen as a result of your gifts—those in need are helped, and they overflow with thanks to God. Those you help will be glad not only because of your generous gifts to themselves and to others, but they will praise God for this proof that your deeds are as good as your doctrine. And they will pray for you with deep fervour and feeling because of the wonderful grace of God shown through you. (2 Corinthians 9: 11–14, TLB)

JOBS

People need jobs, Father.

In work is security:
The means
    to feed and clothe and house our families,
    to educate them,
    to provide pleasures and surprises;
And purpose:
A calling
    to explore our gifts,
    to grow our talents,
    to contribute to the community.

We're accustomed to unemployment,
    as businesses fail,
    jobs are redesigned,
    immigrants arrive,
    young people graduate …
But this is different:
Millions are out of work,
Not because of isolated failures or choices,
But because of this virus.
Perhaps in their need
They will find
    new pathways,
    new directions,
    new careers,
Be open to new callings.

Jesus told stories about employment,
About workers seeking security and purpose.
Yet when he called,
People left their work to follow him.
His call became their calling.
And even today,
People hear your call,
Leave their work to follow you.
Your call becomes their calling,
And they find new meanings
    to security
    and purpose.

Have I found my calling, Father?
Have I heard your call?
Am I serving you where you call me to be?

Work hard and cheerfully at all you do, just as though you were working for the Lord and not merely for your masters, remembering that it is the Lord Christ who is going to pay you, giving you your full portion of all he owns. (Colossians 3: 23–25, TLB)

CHANGED

We are changed, Father.

Things are not the same—
Will not be the same—
Ever.
We have been challenged to think differently
    about our security,
    our health,
    our employment,
    our recreation,
    our travel,
    our way of life,
    our family,
    our priorities,
    our ways of relating …
Unexpected events
Changed our world,
Which changed us:
    what we think,
    what we do,
    what we trust,
    what we plan and dream and hope.
Our world is changed,
Never to be the same again;
So we are changed,
Never to be the same again.
It was the same when I became aware of you, Father—
When I accepted a relationship with Jesus

That led me into communion with you.
I was changed
Never to be the same again;
So my world was changed,
Never to be the same again.

When someone becomes a Christian, he becomes a brand new person inside. He is not the same anymore. A new life has begun! (2 Corinthians 5: 17, TLB)

EASY

It was never going to be easy, Father.

We thought this would be over quickly.
Just a little inconvenience,
　　then life would be normal again.
Don't worry.
It will be easy.

We are so easily convinced,
　　easily persuaded,
　　easily deceived,
By the ignorant and fraudulent;
Those who tempt us with the easy way
To the easy life
And the easy conscience.

Jesus didn't do that, Father.
He didn't tempt people with an easy way,
　　or an easy life,
　　or an easy conscience.
He told us it would be difficult
To love as he loved,
To serve as he served,
To live as he lived.

Am I tempted by the easy way, Father—
The easy way of following Christ,
The easy way of serving you,

The easy way of helping others,
The easy way of living?

Don't look for shortcuts to God. The market is flooded with sure-fire, easy-going formulas for a successful life that can be practised in your spare time. Don't fall for that stuff, even though crowds of people do. The way to life—to God!—is vigorous and requires total attention. (Matthew 7: 13–14, MSG)

RECREATION

They're wanting more recreation, Father.

They want to enjoy
    gyms,
    parks,
    skate parks,
    festivals,
    sport—
Even to *watch* sport would be enough for some.
They need their recreation.

For earlier generations,
Recreation was a novelty,
A rare opportunity in the business of survival.
It continues so for many throughout the world.
But we are lucky.
Recreation is part of our daily timetable.
We demand our recreation,
Moments to re-energise.

You, Father, offer us even better—
Re-creation.
Not simply a moment to be re-energised,
But a lifetime to be renewed,
    re-created,
    re-born
In Christ.

Jesus answered, 'I am telling you the truth: no one can see the Kingdom of God without being born again.' (John 3: 3, GNT)

So get rid of your old self, which made you live as you used to—the old self that was being destroyed by its deceitful desires. Your hearts and minds must be made completely new, and you must put on the new self, which is created in God's likeness and reveals itself in the true life that is upright and holy. (Ephesians 4: 22–24, GNT)

BACK TO SCHOOL

The kids are back at school, Father.

Amid the worry, we celebrate:
    they see friends again;
    they have access to skilled educators;
    their education is reignited;
    their schooling is back on track;
    (and home is quieter!)
But most of all,
It's a return to normality,
To the routine of our lives.

We like routine, Father:
To know
    what to expect,
    what to do,
    when and how.

Yet when we live for you,
We live with surprise.
We cannot know
    what opportunities you will present,
    who we will meet,
    what you will call us to do.
We cannot know
    what to expect,
    what to do,
    when or how.

Reflections on faith inspired by Covid   Phil Ridden

Am I ready, Father,
Constantly watching for you
And the surprises you have for me?

May Jesus himself and God our Father, who reached out in love and surprised you with gifts of unending help and confidence, put a fresh heart in you, invigorate your work, enliven your speech. (2 Thessalonians 2: 16–17, MSG)

SOON

Soon all will be well, Father.

Soon students will all return to school;
Soon the shops will reopen;
Soon children will play in parks and playgrounds;
Soon we will gather with family and friends;
Soon we will meet in church buildings;
Soon we will watch sport or visit the cinema;
Soon the jobs will return;
Soon the isolation will be over;
Soon the fear will be gone;
Soon our lives will return to normal;
Soon ...

It's what we look forward to,
    yearn for,
    hope for.
Yet soon is an unknown time,
A distant event we cannot define.
Soon conspires with anticipation,
Soon shares insights with optimism,
Soon links arms with hope.

In you is the greatest hope, Father.
And soon doesn't matter.
It's enough to know that
Your promises,
Your love,

Are mine
Now.
Anything else will be soon enough.

So we're not giving up. How could we! Even though on the outside it often looks like things are falling apart on us, on the inside, where God is making new life, not a day goes by without his unfolding grace. These hard times are small potatoes compared to the coming good times, the lavish celebration prepared for us. There's far more here than meets the eye. The things we see now are here today, gone tomorrow. But the things we can't see now will last forever. (2 Corinthians 4: 16–18, MSG)

HISTORY

We've been reminded of the history of this virus, Father.

The press displayed a timeline,
Showing how each phase of Covid-19 evolved,
And the national and international response,
From the first reported case
    through to the latest plans.
It reminds us
    where we have come from,
    how we have progressed,
    the decisions our leaders have made,
    the things the people have done,
    and where we are now.
There are events and moments
    to regret,
    to mourn,
    to celebrate,
    to be thankful for,
    to hope for.

In the Bible, Father,
We read how your leaders—
    Moses, Joshua, Ezra, Paul and others—
Reminded the people of their history:
    of how you reached out to them
    and they reached out to you;
Recalled the story:
    of where they had come from,

    how they had progressed,
    the decisions the leaders had made,
    the things the people had done,
    and where they were now;
Reminded them of events and moments:
    to regret,
    to mourn,
    to celebrate,
    to be thankful for,
    to hope for.

It's true for me, too, Father.
I can reflect on my faith history:
How I reached out to you,
    and you reached out to me;
How my faith began,
    and how you have led me to now.
Thank you for the past, Father.
Where next?

As I was travelling and coming near Damascus, about midday a bright light from the sky flashed suddenly around me. I fell to the ground and heard a voice saying to me, 'Saul, Saul! Why do you persecute me?' 'Who are you, Lord?' I asked. 'I am Jesus of Nazareth, whom you persecute,' he said to me. (Acts 22: 6–8, GNT)

PRIORITIES

We've been forced to review our priorities, Father.

Many people have been challenged
By the isolation,
The change of routine,
By the need to adapt:
    to work differently,
    to shop differently,
    to find alternative recreation and entertainment,
    to connect with friends and family differently,
    to find ways to entertain children …

For many, it's been difficult.
Yet it's been an opportunity:
    to discard the things we don't need in our lives,
    to identify what really matters,
    to re-prioritise,
    to stay close to the things that bring us joy.

Do I need to do that, Father?
Have I cluttered my life with things and events?
You gave me life fulfilled,
Life at its richest and best.
Do I cloud that richness,
With …
Things?

So don't worry at all about having enough food and clothing. Why be like the heathen? For they take pride in all these things and are deeply concerned about them. But your heavenly Father already knows perfectly well that you need them, and he will give them to you if you give him first place in your life and live as he wants you to. (Matthew 6: 31–33, TLB)

OPENING

The church doors are opening, Father.

How could it be,
Your churches—closed?

Perhaps it was a good thing:
Perhaps we have given too much attention
    to the trappings of faith;
Perhaps we have been distracted by buildings;
Perhaps we have obsessed about ornaments;
Perhaps we have centred our faith on symbols.

We are your Church,
And your Church was not closed;
Your Church **is** not closed;
Your Church **will never** be closed.
We have been here—
And we will continue to be here—
Sharing the Good News Jesus taught us;
Living the way Jesus showed us;
Serving others as Jesus urged us;
Following Jesus and worshipping you.
The Church is central,
But the building is peripheral.

Keep me always, Father,
Living in you,
Connected with your family,

And being the Church—
Even when health,
> or age,
> or location,
> or rules,
Keep me from church.

To: *The Christians in Corinth, invited by God to be his people and made acceptable to him by Christ Jesus.* And to: *All Christians everywhere—whoever calls upon the name of Jesus Christ, our Lord and theirs. May God our Father and the Lord Jesus Christ give you all of his blessings, and great peace of heart and mind. (1 Corinthians 1: 2–3, TLB)*

LOCKDOWN

They're opening the borders, Father.

For a time we were in lockdown.
Citizens could return home from overseas,
But no visitors were allowed.
Our country was closed for business.
Even our state borders were closed,
And then regional boundaries closed.
Our freedom to travel,
Taken for granted,
Was gone,
And we were locked down in one place.

Sometimes I feel my faith is like that, Father.
I want to explore new places,
    new visions
    new challenges,
    new experiences,
    new opportunities,
    new understandings,
    new ways of seeing the world—
Through faith;
But instead, I'm locked down in one place.

Will you help me travel, Father?
To explore new ways to know you,
    new ways to be faithful,
    new ways to serve,

    new ways to love,
    new ways to be;
To continually seek
Newness?

So don't you see that we don't owe this old do-it-yourself life one red cent. There's nothing in it for us, nothing at all. The best thing to do is give it a decent burial and get on with your new life. God's Spirit beckons. There are things to do and places to go! This resurrection life you received from God is not a timid, grave-tending life. It's adventurously expectant, greeting God with a childlike 'What's next, Papa?' God's Spirit touches our spirits and confirms who we really are. (Romans 8: 12–15, MSG)

SECOND WAVE

We were warned of the second wave, Father.

We endured the first wave—
    obeyed the rules,
    followed the guidelines,
    patiently restricted our contacts,
Until we appeared to have this virus defeated.
But the moment we relaxed,
    became less vigilant,
    invited people across our borders,
    re-united with our social networks,
Then came the second wave—
    a new wave of infections,
    a new threat to all of us,
    a new imposition of restrictions.

It is so easy to allow ourselves to be duped,
    to become apathetic—
And we suffer the consequences.

Jesus warned us that our faith was like this, Father.
In his story,
As the sower threw the seed,
Some fell on rocky ground—
Finding soil in which to germinate,
It grew quickly;
But its roots had no depth,
And when the heat scorched it,

It withered and died.

The seed of faith may germinate
And grow quickly,
But if its roots have no depth,
When the heat of life scorches it,
It will wither and die.

Let me find depth in my faith, Father—
Roots that are secured deep in you,
Drawing life from deep in Jesus,
Able to withstand the scorching
Of whatever heat I may feel.

The farmer plants the Word. ... And some are like the seed that lands in the gravel. When they first hear the Word, they respond with great enthusiasm. But there is such shallow soil of character that when the emotions wear off and some difficulty arrives, there is nothing to show for it. (Mark 4: 13, 16–17, MSG)

FACE TO FACE

We have come face to face, Father.

Face to face with death;
Face to face with despair;
Face to face with fear;
Face to face with uncertainty …
And in such moments,
When we have had nothing left to fall back on,
We have come face to face with you.
Some who have never used your name,
    except in profanity,
Have called to you.

When we come face to face with you, Father,
We come face to faith with you.
We ask for so much,
    but expect so little.
We look for Jesus,
    but turn away when we see him.
We plead for your help,
    but commend ourselves on our success.

I've come face to face with new experiences, Father.
Let me come face to face with you—
Your love,
Your grace,
Your peace …

Jesus spoke to her, 'Woman, why do you weep? Who are you looking for?' She, thinking that he was the gardener, said, 'Mister, if you took him, tell me where you put him so I can care for him.' Jesus said, 'Mary.' Turning to face him, she said in Hebrew, 'Rabboni!' meaning 'Teacher!' (John 20: 15–16, MSG)

PROTECTED

They have found a vaccine, Father.

We are protected from this virus.
Even without our awareness,
It may be near us,
    but it cannot breach our defences.
It may touch us,
    but it cannot hurt us.
It may invade our body,
    but we are immune from its influence.
When we attend a clinic,
Allow doctors to inject us with this essence,
We are inoculated,
Protected from the dangers of this virus.

We have a vaccine against evil, too Father.
Even without our awareness,
It may be near us,
    but it cannot breach our defences.
It may touch us,
    but it cannot hurt us.
It may invade our body,
    but we are immune from its influence.
When we come to you,
Allow you to fill us with your Spirit,
We are protected,
Held safe in your care.

Keep your eye on the healthy soul, scrutinise the straight life; There's a future in strenuous wholeness. But the wilful will soon be discarded; insolent souls are on a dead-end street. The spacious, free life is from GOD, it's also protected and safe. GOD-strengthened, we're delivered from evil—when we run to him, he saves us. (Psalm 37: 37–40, MSG)

TEST

We have a test for infection, Father.

A simple test can detect an elevated temperature,
Which might mean infection.
It takes a moment;
No contact required.
A more thorough test
Can detect infection by the virus.
It takes a little longer;
Some saliva or mucous required.

I'm infected, Father—
Infected with your love,
Infused with your Spirit.
But can it be detected by others?
Is it evident at a glance?
Does it take a little longer to see?
Or is it hidden, masked,
So that no-one is aware?

Is your life,
Evident in my life
For all to see?

Don't hide your light! Let it shine for all; let your good deeds glow for all to see, so that they will praise your heavenly Father. (Matthew 5: 15–16, TLB)

PUBLIC TRANSPORT

They're shunning public transport, Father.

There is risk on the trains and buses,
Risk of infection from a random stranger,
Seated uncomfortably close.
So they travel in cars,
    safe,
    alone.

I understand, Father.
Sometimes I use public transport,
Sometimes I prefer my car.
Even beyond Covid,
There are many reasons
    why I choose to travel alone;
There are many reasons
    why I choose to travel with others;
But there is never a reason to travel
Without you.

Calling the crowd to join his disciples, he said, 'Anyone who intends to come with me has to let me lead. You're not in the driver's seat; I am. Don't run from suffering; embrace it. Follow me and I'll show you how. Self-help is no help at all. Self-sacrifice is the way, my way, to saving yourself, your true self.' (Mark 8: 34–35, MSG)

IT'S OVER

To the reader:

At the time of publication, the Covid-19 virus is still rampant in many countries, impacting people's lives in a variety of ways, and continuing to cause death.

This book cannot be completed at this time. So now it's up to you. If, as you read this, the Covid virus continues to cause distress, reflect on how you think you will feel and respond when it is defeated. If the crisis is over, reflect on how you feel now.

Then why not write your own reflection on faith? Perhaps you will share it with others and with me.

Phil Ridden
Phil@philridden.biz

By the same author:

Reflections on faith inspired by babies
Reflections on faith inspired by children
Reflections on faith inspired by seniors
Reflections on faint inspired by men
Faith around the barbecue (The story)
Faith around the barbecue (The play)

Search: www.philridden.biz

www.ingramcontent.com/pod-product-compliance
Lightning Source LLC
Chambersburg PA
CBHW070432010526
44118CB00014B/2010